Business Communication Pocket Guide

Practical Presentation Skills

Authenticity, Focus & Strength

Brandt Johnson

ALEY

This edition published in 2019 by Nicholas Brealey Publishing
An imprint of John Murray Press

An Hachette UK company

23 22 21 20 19   1 2 3 4 5 6 7 8 9 10

A CIP catalogue record for this title is available from the British
Library.

Library of Congress Control Number: 2019939681

ISBN 978-1-52930-344-5
US eBook ISBN 978-1-52930-358-2
UK eBook ISBN 978-1-52930-343-8

Printed and bound in the United States of America.

John Murray Press policy is to use papers that are natural, renewable,
and recyclable products and made from wood grown in sustainable
forests. The logging and manufacturing processes are expected to
conform to the environmental regulations of the country of origin.

John Murray Press Ltd   Nicholas Brealey Publishing
Carmelite House   Hachette Book Group
50 Victoria Embankment   53 State Street
London EC4Y 0DZ   Boston, MA 02109, USA
Tel: 020 3122 6000   Tel: (617) 263 1834

www.nbuspublishing.com

Contents

Introduction

A Broad Perspective

Y ou give presentations all the time. Whenever you are talking to someone, or to a group of people, you are presenting yourself and your ideas to an audience.

That audience may be your colleagues, clients, or people you haven't met before. You may be sitting, standing, or walking down a hallway. You may be in a cubicle or a boardroom. You may be speaking in person, on the phone, or via videoconference.

Regardless of the scenario, when you are presenting yourself and your ideas to an audience, you are giving a presentation.

When you are giving a presentation, both your content and your delivery contribute to the vitality and effectiveness of your message.

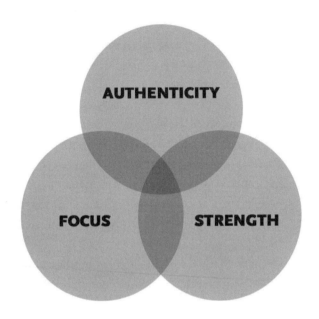

This book covers many diverse aspects of content and delivery, but they represent three fundamental elements of effective communication: authenticity, focus, and strength. When a presentation has all three of these elements, it has its greatest chance for success.

- *Authenticity.* By showing your true personality and demonstrating genuine interest in your content and your listeners, you will draw your audience in. When you allow your authentic self to be seen, you invite your audience to have a unique (literally, one-of-a-kind) experience. There is only one you. There are countless speakers who pretend and perform, who try to play some business role they think people want to see—there is a bland sameness to that. However, there is an exciting and vibrant singularity in you, whoever you really are. Share it with your audience. Be yourself.

- *Focus.* Focus heightens your awareness, clarifies your purpose, and gives you direction. You need to focus not only on what you are trying to accomplish but also on your listeners and what they need.

- *Strength.* Many factors, including body language, voice, and the quality of your content, influence the strength of your presence. The stronger your presence, the more engaging you will be, and the more confidence you will inspire in your listeners.

Two types of sidebars appear throughout the book: Notes from the Workplace and Terrible Tips: Advice to Ignore.

Notes from the Workplace are real-life observations drawn primarily from my experience working with corporate executives and others as a communication skills consultant. To ensure the anonymity of the people who appear in these segments, I have changed names, contexts, and other identifying features. In some cases, I have combined aspects of more than one scenario into a single story. When I refer to workshops, I'm talking about the presentation skills workshops I conduct for clients.

Terrible Tips: Advice to Ignore is a collection of misguided and perplexingly common pieces of bad advice that are floating around the corporate world and interfering with effective communication. Beware of terrible tips.

In the Appendix, checklists for each chapter highlight key points and provide a convenient reference to help refresh your memory.

This book is written primarily from an American business perspective. Of course, it is crucial to be sensitive to the various cultural contexts of your listeners and how those contexts may influence what they appreciate in a communication.

Happy reading!

Brandt W.

Chapter 1

Authenticity

Authenticity is the essential core of an effective communication—in any context, personal or professional.

1.1 Establishing a Connection

If you give people around you the sense that you are for real, that what they are seeing and hearing is genuinely you, they will be more likely to believe you, care about you and your ideas, and participate in a communication with you.

If, on the other hand, they don't feel that you are being authentic, no matter how technically perfect your presentation, there will be a distance between you and them that will be very difficult to bridge. A presentation can survive all sorts of shortcomings and mistakes, but a lack of authenticity in the content or delivery is lethal to a meaningful connection with your listeners.

Companies are collections of people, and people respond to connections with other people. Business happens human being to human being.

It's easy to get distracted from this basic point

amidst the pressures of getting things right when the stakes are high. Don't get distracted.

1.2 Authenticity vs. Professionalism

People want to behave professionally in the workplace. They want to convey a sense that they are taking their jobs and the moment at hand seriously.

Often this means that they shift away from their natural personalities. To varying degrees, they contain themselves and become less naturally expressive as they play the part of what they think is a professional person.

The problem is that being less *you* does not make you more professional. It makes you less interesting, less believable, less inspiring, and less likely to motivate listeners to consider your ideas. It makes you less powerful.

The more *you* in the room, the better.

Listeners, whether they know you or not, can sense when you are performing instead of being genuine. They can sense when you are trying to be someone you are not, forcing yourself into a false mold. But they can also sense when you are genuinely present.

People receiving your ideas in the workplace are

not hoping for some polished, perfect performance. They want a message that matters to them, delivered in a way that makes really good use of their time, coming from someone who is truly connected to them and the content.

Unfortunately, the perspectives of speakers and listeners are often misaligned from the start.

Speakers can obsess about the very stuff that doesn't matter to anyone else. To a speaker, it can feel so important to get everything just right, to deliver a perfect performance that has no stumbles or rough edges at all. No one else cares. (See 6.1: Your Perspective.)

In fact, some imperfection can actually draw listeners closer as they think, "Hey, I'm imperfect, too. We have that in common!" (See 6.4: Imperfection.)

✎ Notes from the Workplace ✎

Being Professional

I was coaching an investment banker named Willard who had recently taken on a more senior position at his firm and was meeting more frequently with potential clients.

Willard was highly confident in his technical understanding of finance, but he wasn't feeling comfortable in these meetings.

1

He thought that in order to be seen as professional in his new role, he needed to buff away any bumps or grooves in his personality and present his listeners with a smooth veneer. But the more he adopted his glossy approach, the less he engaged his audience.

Once Willard became fully aware of what was happening, he was able to shed his false persona. During our final coaching session, tears welled up in his eyes as he described the freedom and power he felt from just being himself.

1.3 What's Natural for You

Developing your communication style is similar in some ways to learning to play a sport or musical instrument. A coach might suggest an adjustment to your stroke, grip, or stance. A teacher might recommend another way of striking the keys, strumming the strings, or blowing into the mouthpiece.

At first, the adjustment might feel unnatural. But after trying it out and practicing, you may well find that the new way really helps. You may decide to adopt it as your own.

We can continue to be true to ourselves while we explore and expand our perspectives and ways of doing things. If we stay open to change, our self-perceptions can shift to include infinite and forever-evolving versions of ourselves. This is an ongoing process.

1.4 Selling

Some meetings and phone calls with salespeople feel like pitches while others don't. Some salespeople come off as salesy while others don't.

Why?

Let's consider two salespeople.

George: Salesy

George has as his primary objective making a sale and making it right away. If it turns out well for the client, great. If not, well, at least the deal closed. George vigorously challenges every objection, repeats his main message, and pushes to get agreements. George uses the tips and tricks he has learned to manipulate his prospective clients into buying what he is selling.

Blythe: Not Salesy

Blythe has as her primary objective serving her potential clients. She wants to find solutions to their problems and develop relationships with them. She listens to their concerns and misgivings. She expresses herself genuinely and openly. This establishes a context from which sales—and repeat sales—will more likely emerge over the long run.

Of course, both George and Blythe want to

consummate deals. They need to make sales in order to keep their jobs. But focusing exclusively on the thing you want to happen can actually get in the way of its happening.

George's shortsighted push to make sales now sacrifices longer-term and more profitable relationships. When people feel pressured or manipulated, they often retreat rather than engage. And even if he can overpower them in the moment and get them to sign the deal, they may experience a lingering unease once he leaves the room or hangs up the phone. This will get in the way of a continuing relationship.

Blythe, on the other hand, maintains a broader perspective. She understands that today's interaction is an opportunity to strengthen her relationship with the potential client, regardless of the immediate outcome. Blythe knows that respecting boundaries is key to a lasting relationship. Since people appreciate Blythe's authentic and responsive way of communicating, they will be more willing to take her calls in the future.

1.5 Truth

Stories abound about people who have won business deals (or romantic dates) by shading the truth.

Misrepresentation can present itself as a seductive shortcut in those moments when the only thing standing between you and what you want is the truth. And it may indeed get you what you want in those moments. But it will fail you in the long run.

If you tell untruths, at some point some of them will be discovered. If you misrepresented yourself to me last time, it's unlikely I'll give you an opportunity for a next time. Integrity is an indispensable element of what you can offer people on the other side of a communication with you.

Maintaining your integrity is good business. It's also just a more satisfying and meaningful way to live your life.

Chapter 2

Content

The most important thing you can do with your content is engage your listeners. If they don't care, not much else matters.

What engages them? It depends on who they are and what their relationship is to your topic. The same topic can be presented in many different ways depending on who the audience is.

2.1 Audience

An outward focus on the needs and interests of the people listening to you is central to making your communication a success.

- What does your audience know?
- What don't they know?
- What do they want to know?
- What don't they want to know?
- What matters most to them?
- How sophisticated are they?
- How can you make it as easy as possible for them to understand your ideas?
- What will make the best use of their time?

Answering these questions will help ensure that your message is relevant, clear, and valuable to your audience.

2.2 Knowing Your Content

If you want your audience to engage with your content, you need to engage with it yourself. Take the time to really understand what you are going to say and why. Make sure your objectives are clear in your mind.

What about the content is meaningful to you? Your message will be most compelling at the intersection of what matters to your listeners and what matters to you.

When you are first developing your content, try not to censor yourself too much. Let your ideas flow freely—the good ones as well as the not-so-good ones—without judging them. This will leave your mind open so you can be your most creative, original self.

2.3 The Beginning

Beginning is one of the most difficult things to do in life. You are making a transition from not doing something to doing it, and that can be an especially challenging moment. Presentations are no exception.

But the beginning of a presentation also offers a significant opportunity. There is a high degree of focus on you when you are just about to speak. People are sizing you up, wondering what you are about to say and whether it will be worthwhile. You can take advantage of that opportunity by opening your mouth and engaging your listeners with your very first words.

Don't make people wait to be glad to be listening to you. Make them glad right away.

When you prepare a strong beginning, you are not only serving the audience but also giving yourself something to rely on, to feel confident about as you start speaking. (See 6.3: Preparation.)

Your very early content should accomplish two primary objectives:

1. It should engage your listeners.
2. It should give them a sense of what's to come.

Often beginnings focus only on the second objective. For example, a speaker may lay out every topic and subtopic of a presentation in bullet-point form and read through it all in monotonous detail.

Instead, for a beginning that achieves both objectives, try touching immediately on one or more of the most engaging aspects of your message. Where in your topic is the spark for your listeners? What insights might you share? Trust that your listeners are smart enough to infer the subject of your talk from what you're saying—without your having to say things like "I'm going to speak to you about…"

There are innumerable ways to craft an effective beginning. As you are writing your opening, consider not only the character of your audience but also your own personality. What style suits you best?

You could start with a relevant anecdote. Stories can provide a wealth of vivid details to help capture listeners' attention. The story form has captivated audiences since the dawn of human communication.

Beginning with a question can also draw listeners into your talk. However, if your question is not rhetorical—that is, if it calls for an answer—then you should use this approach only if you are very confident that you'll get a response. Sometimes people don't want to play along when they're asked a question. You should also be prepared to use to your advantage whatever comes back from the audience.

Yet another way to start is with the opposite of a question: a statement. It might be your primary theme or the distillation of certain key elements of your presentation. It could be market data or a striking statistic or fact. A strong statement can give the audience an immediate and specific idea of the nature of the topic and why it is important.

Resist the temptation to start by telling everyone how much work you put into the presentation and how excited you are. Your audience expects that you put effort into it. And instead of hearing that you are excited, they would rather hear a good idea that excites them.

Furthermore, avoid dumping all of your resume items and your firm's credentials on your listeners as you first start speaking. Some speakers think they need to do this in order to establish credibility.

Credibility is not a bad thing to establish. But starting off with a list of reasons you think you're great is not the best way to do it. Instead, inspire confidence in your listeners by demonstrating that you understand them and that you are focused in a smart, creative way on what they care about most.

Sometimes speakers begin by unnecessarily pointing out deficiencies in the presentation they're about to give. This highlights weaknesses the listeners may not otherwise have been aware of, and it can distract from the presentation's strengths. Perhaps these speakers feel that if they criticize themselves first it will inoculate them from the audience's criticism later on. It won't.

Finally, you can skip telling listeners that you know their time is valuable (which is, paradoxically, a waste of time) and that you won't take much of it. Instead, show them that you value their time by starting with ideas that make good use of it.

It's not the duration of a presentation that matters most; it's the quality. If you make good use of your listeners' time, they will be happy you are using it. If not, they won't—no matter how little of it you waste. (See 2.7: Time.)

Examples of Beginnings

Imagine a scenario where you are seeking investments in your firm's marquee project, Project Shmoject. You had a conference call yesterday with prospective investors, and they told you they won't invest unless the name of the project is changed.

You need to present this issue at a meeting of your firm's executive committee. Let's consider a few possible approaches to the beginning of your presentation.

Common Business Beginning (not recommended)

I am going to talk about Project Shmoject. An issue has come up that we need to consider.

Alternative 1: Anecdote

I spoke with prospective investors in Project Shmoject yesterday. They told me if we don't change the name, they won't invest.

Alternative 2: Statement

The name "Project Shmoject" is driving away investors.

Alternative 3: Question

Are we willing to lose investors in order to keep the name "Project Shmoject"?

The common business beginning above is rather vague and uninformative. This leaves the executive committee waiting to hear specifics about why they should care.

Alternatives 1, 2, and 3 get more immediately into the substance of the topic, giving the executive committee something to care about right away and setting a clear direction for the content. Of course, in each of these cases your presentation would continue, expanding on your initial ideas.

There are many ways you could begin, but in the best case, you won't wait to pique your listeners' interest and give them a sense of what's to come.

Make Time to Think About Your Beginning

You may be overbooked and running from meeting to meeting. You may feel as though you don't have enough time to prepare a beginning.

But you do.

You can always take even just a minute or two at some point to stop and think about your beginning. What can you say to engage your listeners and give your talk direction? The difference between not preparing at all and preparing even just a little bit is enormous.

⊘ Terrible Tips: Advice to Ignore ⊘

Start with a joke to "break the ice."

Professional comedians fail at comedy all the time. For amateur joke tellers, the risk of failure is higher still. Getting the structure, tone, and timing just right so that a joke is actually funny to your audience is very hard to do. A failed joke will distract your listeners from your message and may also make them feel uncomfortable.

Furthermore, many speakers just aren't at ease when they're trying to be funny. When they try anyway, because someone told them they should start with a joke, it can seem forced—and unfunny.

If the goal of "breaking the ice" is to establish a connection with your listeners, there are far more reliable and less contrived ways to do it than by telling a joke.

Of course, it's possible to tell a joke that works. If you're naturally funny, the content of your joke is relevant to your topic, and you're able to tell it in a way that your audience finds funny, then it could work.

But when jokes feel forced and fake, as they so often do in business settings, it's a painful experience for everyone involved.

Effective humor more often finds its way into presentations in non-joke form, as spontaneous asides or funny connections or observations made in the moment by a freely expressive speaker who is being natural and showing some personality.

People like to laugh. When humor arrives, it can feel like a gift from the speaker. "Oh, thank you very much! Hahahaha!"

However, you don't need to be funny to be effective. The most important thing is to be yourself.

Don't ever say you're sorry.

Some people think saying they're sorry shows weakness. It's true that frequent and unnecessary apologies will diminish your standing in a communication. However, there are plenty of situations that legitimately call for an apology—keeping a group waiting because you were running late, for example.

One of my workshop participants advocated saying "I appreciate your patience" when showing up late, rather than apologizing. But people you inconvenience may actually be annoyed and not patient at all. Telling them they're patient won't help. It will just annoy them further.

If you don't apologize when you should, you will put a distance between yourself and your listeners, which will weaken your ability to get your message across.

2.4 Clarity

As you proceed through your presentation, maintain your outward focus on your audience's experience, and be sure you are making the content clear and easy for them to understand.

What's clear to some people may not be clear to others. Formulate your content to match your listeners' familiarity with your topic and their degree of sophistication. If you confuse your audience, it becomes much more likely that you will lose their attention.

In order to help your listeners understand your content, you need to understand it yourself. If your ideas are meandering in your own head, they're going to meander their way out of your mouth.

Help the audience follow your train of thought by organizing your ideas logically and using examples where appropriate.

Value simplicity. Avoid overly ornate sentence structures and accumulations of dense ideas. Too much complexity will prevent people from keeping up. Consider reiterating your most important points over the course of your presentation to ensure that they register with the audience.

At any time during a presentation, if you need to take a moment to gain some clarity in your own mind, take it. Pause. Consider what your listeners need. Feel free to check in with them to make sure they are still following you.

✎ Notes from the Workplace ✎

Trying to Say Too Much

A young lawyer named Olivia was asked to organize a panel discussion for her firm's annual conference. There were five panelists, including Olivia. Each person was scheduled to speak for 10 minutes, and the panel could not exceed the total allocated time.

On the day of the panel discussion, just before stepping up to the dais, one of the panelists, a senior partner at Olivia's firm, informed her that he would be speaking for 15 minutes, not 10. That meant Olivia would have to cut her talk time to five minutes.

She had worked very hard on her talk, and it was full of useful information. She didn't want to lose any of it. When it was her turn to speak, she proceeded with the talk she had prepared but delivered it twice as fast.

Then came questions from the audience. It was clear they had not understood much of anything from her portion of the panel. She had provided a lot of great ideas but at a breakneck pace that had not allowed any of those ideas to sink in.

What should Olivia have done? She had limited options. First, she could have told the senior partner no, or cut him off at 10 minutes—probably not a good career move. Since the panel was just about to start, she couldn't very well have told the other panelists to shorten their talks, either.

Therefore, she was forced to limit her own speaking time to five minutes. But she was still free to decide what to do with that shorter time.

Her choice to stick with all of the original content was a mistake. Had she cut the content in half, the audience would have lost out on what she eliminated, yes, but they would have at least been able to digest what she did decide to keep. Instead, the audience lost out on all of it.

2.5 Jargon

Many speakers pepper their talks with jargon. Some of them are trying to sound as though they have inside knowledge of a topic or industry. Others are so steeped in the vocabulary that they're not even aware they're using it. Either way, jargon can put off an audience.

Some jargon is widely understood, so it doesn't cause confusion. But it still sounds trite, as if the speaker got it from some generic retailer's back-aisle shelf of used and returned words. Jargon fails to show the speaker's own original way of formulating an idea, relying instead on a prefabricated, tired design.

Other jargon is not widely understood and does cause confusion. Confusing an audience with jargon doesn't make them feel impressed that the speaker knows some insider code. It makes them feel less connected to the presentation and more likely to disengage.

Use your own language. Consider your ideas and express them naturally, whatever that means for you. This will bring your own expressiveness, connection to the content, and personality to the communication. That's something your listeners can relate to.

2.6 Conciseness

If you can say something in fewer words, do.

People don't complain when talks or meetings are shorter and more efficient than they expected. But speakers sometimes feel the need to fill time, measuring their worth in quantity of words rather than precision of ideas.

You can't ever say everything there is to say about a topic. In any context, you need to choose; you need to curate the vast store of potential information you could potentially include in a talk. Then you need to interpret, distill, and give your audience their best chance to understand and relate to your ideas. When you are giving an effective presentation, you are both curator and interpreter.

It's much more difficult to formulate focused, concise thoughts than to pour out large volumes of content. But it's worth the effort. Your listeners will appreciate it.

Develop your ideas with enough specificity to bring them to life but not so many details that your larger message gets lost. This can be a delicate balance to strike.

So many presentations suffocate under an avalanche of data and details. Others suffer from broad generalities that offer listeners nothing specific to grab hold of. Exercise your own judgment and give enough but not too much.

Imagine you're in a meeting and a senior executive asks you to give her a brief summary of your opinion on a potential deal. Here are three alternative approaches to your response:

1: Too Much Detail

In our analysis of the deal, we assumed that revenue will increase 15.4 percent per year for the first two years, 17.5 percent in year 3, 18.1 percent in year 4, and 22.7 percent per year in years 5 through 10. Costs are projected to remain unchanged in year 1 but decrease by 6.3 percent per year in years 2 through 10, enhancing cash flow growth. We analyzed the deal using five different sets of assumptions, ranging from the worst case to the best case. Returns were 11.8 percent in case 1, 15.2 percent in case 2, 16.1 percent in case 3, 17.4 percent in case 4, and 18.9 percent in case 5. I recommend that we do the deal.

2: Not Enough Detail

I think it's a really good deal. I like it. We should do it.

3: Enough Detail but Not Too Much

We expect revenue growth and cost savings to result in significantly increased cash flow over the next 10 years. Based on our assumptions, the return on our investment would be in the range of 15 to 18 percent. We should do the deal.

If the executive wants more detail, she can ask for it.

2.7 Time

Time is perhaps our most precious resource. We get only so much of it each day, and we get only a limited number of days. Each of us will run out of time at some point, and every moment that passes is gone forever, never to be recovered. Time is a wasting asset.

You have less left now than when you began reading this sentence.

Of course, this is all true in any context, but our perspective on time is quite different in professional settings than in our personal lives. When we get together with friends or loved ones, we spend time without a careful cataloguing of what value accrues from that expenditure. We just spend it, freely, because it feels good to be with people we like.

In our professional lives, on the other hand, time is more carefully guarded, measured, and valued. Time is currency. When we spend that currency, we hope it will yield something valuable beyond having a good time.

There is never enough time to do everything we want to do. We have to choose, and each choice is at the expense of every other option. When people spend their time on you, when they stop and listen to what you have to say, make it count. Make it worth their time.

By demonstrating that you are a responsible steward of people's time, you will make them glad to give it to you. They will appreciate the care you take with their treasured, limited resource.

Conversely, being careless with people's time is a sure way to put distance between you and them. Think about the occasions when someone made poor use of your time. What did you experience in those moments? That feeling is pervasive in the workplace. In meeting after meeting, all over the world, time is squandered.

Some people speak for the sake of speaking. Others ramble, unable to get to the point or say what they mean. It's frustrating. It's annoying. This wasting of time is a hallmark of many business interactions.

If you can be the person who stands in stark contrast to the corporate time-wasters, if you are the one who cuts through the fog and bloat of typical business interactions, who takes less time than expected, finishes early, gets people what they need efficiently and briskly, with purpose and focus, then you will be the one people want to listen to. You will be the one they gladly entrust with the thing they just don't have enough of—their time.

2.8 Flexibility

Preparation is essential, but some speakers get overly attached to the material they prepared. They worked so hard on it! They can't stop themselves from dragging everyone through their slides, even on the occasions when they see that no one cares. Don't be one of those speakers.

Stop.

Listen.

Respond to the verbal and nonverbal cues your audience is sending you. Throw away everything you prepared and redirect your presentation, if necessary, to make it a valuable use of your listeners' time.

2.9 Beware of Bad Writing!

At some point, you may be asked to deliver someone else's mediocre presentation, complete with speaker notes. If that happens, focus on the ideas that need to be conveyed, not on the words the last person chose to use. Make the presentation your own.

2.10 Beware of Good Writing!

It's easy to fall in love with your own beautifully written sentence. But sometimes written words don't translate well to spoken form. They can sound unnatural, as though they were meant to be written, not spoken. Pay attention to this risk.

If you've written words you plan to say, say them out loud ahead of time. See how they feel coming out of your mouth. Is that how you speak normally? Does it feel conversational? Your reliance on scripted words should be extremely limited (see 6.3: Preparation).

The more naturally conversational your presentation

is, the more engaging it will be. People respond to people who are being themselves.

2.11 The Conclusion

What do you want to leave your listeners with? What do you want them to be thinking and feeling when you finish speaking? Do you want them to go off and do something? The end is the time to emphasize what matters most.

By the time you reach your conclusion, the audience will be more educated about your topic. You can build on this understanding in your closing. For example, you could consider the implications of your message for the future, or you could ask your audience to do something.

You might incorporate content from your listeners' questions or comments. But you should still prepare ahead of time a clear plan for how to wrap up. Then add to it or deviate from it as necessary.

An effective conclusion to a presentation can feel like the end of a piece of music, where the rhythm carries listeners along to the final resolution. This feeling comes not only from the content, but also from the flow of the delivery.

You can usually avoid having to say, "In conclusion. . ." Just pause before your conclusion and take your time as you leave the audience with the ideas that really matter. Your listeners will get it: you're bringing things to a close.

Whatever last words you choose, give the audience a moment to process your final thoughts before asking for questions, exiting, or otherwise shifting focus away from your conclusion.

2

Chapter 3

Body Language

The tone of a talk is often established physically, with the speaker's entrance into the room or approach to the podium. Once a talk has begun, body language continues to send myriad signals that influence listeners.

3.1 Presenting Is a Physical Activity

You could have just sent an email. Your message could have traveled into your recipients' minds without involving your body at all. Countless authors who no longer even have bodies continue to speak to their readers generation after generation.

But you didn't. You decided to say it out loud. And now your body is involved.

In fact, now your body is a central element of the delivery of your message. Your posture, breathing, and movement will all contribute to or detract from the strength of your ideas.

3.2 Physical Warm-Up Exercises

To prepare your body to express itself, loosen it up and stretch it out. If possible, go to a restroom or other private area shortly before your presentation and do some preparatory exercises. The night before or the morning of your presentation, you may want to try your favorite form of exercise—running, yoga, a game of basketball—as a way of helping you relax.

Below are a few warm-up exercises that can be useful. You may have your own favorites. Whatever you like to do to get loose and physically ready is fine!

- *Neck stretch.* While standing up straight, slowly let your head hang forward so your chin approaches your chest. Don't force it. Rock your head gently from side to side. Return to an upright position.
- *Shoulder rolls.* Roll your shoulders forward, up, and back, stretching them as far as they will go in each direction.
- *Arm swings.* Swing your arms back and forth across your chest.
- *Back and leg stretch.* Standing up straight with your feet about shoulder-width apart, slowly bring your chin down toward your chest and then keep lowering your head slowly toward the floor. Curve your spine one vertebra at a time, bending at the waist with your arms dangling down toward the floor until you feel a stretch in the backs of your legs and your lower back. Don't

force it. From this position, move your torso slowly to the left, reaching for your left foot, and then to your right, reaching for your right foot. Return slowly to an upright position.

- *Wiggles.* Yes, wiggles! Gently wiggle every part of your body, keeping it as loose and relaxed as possible.
- *Making faces.* Contort your face in a variety of ways, using as many of your facial muscles as possible.
- *Yawning.* Open your mouth and yawn.
- *Deep breaths.* Breathe in as far as you possibly can, hold for a moment, and then breathe out—all the way out.

Of course, you may not be able to get to a private place to stretch, wiggle, yawn, etc., before you speak. In that case, you can employ subtle variations of these exercises in whatever way may be appropriate to the setting. For example, in any context you can take a deep breath and let your arms hang loosely by your sides, giving a slight wiggle to your shoulders and wrists to ensure that you're relaxed.

Once you've begun speaking, check in with your body from time to time. The fact that you loosened up before you started your talk doesn't necessarily mean you will stay loose.

By staying aware of what you're doing, you can choose whether you want to continue doing it or make an adjustment. This keeps you from slipping into some default behavior you'd rather not slip into.

Keeping your body relaxed and open to impulse will help your gestures stay free and natural.

3.3 Hands, Feet, and Other Parts

Think of your body in two segments: the foundation (from the waist down) and the upper body (from the waist up).

Let's start with the foundation. Stand with your feet a comfortable distance apart and distribute your weight evenly on both feet, so you are balanced. There is a physical strength and readiness that comes with balance.

When you are not balanced, you are not ready. Imagine standing off-balance on a basketball court, soccer field, or tennis court with someone dribbling toward you or hitting a ball your way. What happens next? Your opponent waltzes by unchecked, or the ball bounces past unreturned.

When you stand with a balanced foundation, you are delivering a subtext that says, "I'm ready." It's simple but powerful.

This doesn't mean you shouldn't move from your spot; feel free to go wherever you like.

What about your upper body? Think of a string attached to your sternum that lifts up to the ceiling. Your shoulders stay nice and loose. Give them a little wiggle to make sure they're not stuck.

Check in with your abdomen. It should be engaged, supporting the rest of your torso. This is the core of your strength. Not stiff but engaged. Think of a dancer's posture: up, open, supple, strong. You can think of yoga or Pilates or whatever else may help you conjure the image of strength combined with flexibility and freedom of movement.

Take a deep breath in, all the way in, and let it out slowly. Release any tension or tightness. Give another wiggle to your shoulders. Stay loose.

Now what about your hands and arms?

Leave them available.

Leave them free to respond naturally to whatever impulses come along. This will also help you maintain an open physical presence, as opposed to clasping your hands in front of you or crossing your arms.

"But I can't just leave my arms alone, dangling there like a couple of overcooked pieces of spaghetti," you might say. Yes, actually, you can. And they won't be hanging around for long, because some impulse to move, however subtle, will arrive, and if you are really available, you will respond.

Maybe you won't gesture much. Maybe you'll engage your hands and arms quite vigorously. That depends on who you are, what you're talking about, etc. But if you let that physical expression flow, you will be your most naturally expressive. You will be your most you. And as previously noted, the more *you* in the room, the better.

3

✎ Notes from the Workplace ✎

Slouching

Samantha, an editor at a major publishing company, stood in front of the group during a workshop, her shoulders slouched. I asked her about her posture, and her response echoed what I have heard from other women.

Some women have reported to me that they don't like to stand (or sit) up straight, because it feels as though they are drawing attention to their chests, which makes them uncomfortable. In workplaces that are primarily male, this uneasiness can be heightened. Therefore they slouch, making themselves a bit smaller, a bit less present, a bit less powerful.

For men and for women, embracing who we are, including our individuality and our physicality, is not always easy. But bringing our full selves to interactions with other people is key to having our ideas received with the strength they deserve.

Samantha tried an adjustment. She engaged her core and lifted herself upward. A power and grace emanated from her new posture as if to say, "I am here."

And she really was.

⊘ Terrible Tips: Advice to Ignore ⊘

Keep your hands in front of you, fingertips touching, in a pyramid position.

Move your hands only for emphasis or to make specific points.

Hold something in your hands to occupy them.

Each of these terrible tips suggests steps to make your hands less available, less natural, and less expressive. This will make you less *you* and in turn make you less engaging and less powerful. Do not heed these terrible tips.

Mirror the physical positions and movements of the person you are talking to.

When people are enjoying each other's company, sometimes they end up mirroring each other's behavior without even realizing it. That's natural.

However, consciously mirroring people in an effort to get them to feel more comfortable with you is disingenuous and problematic.

First, it's not arising naturally from a connection between you and the person you're talking to.

Rather, it's an attempt to force a connection, and it may well feel forced to the other person.

Second, just because the person you are meeting with is tipped back in a chair with feet up on the table doesn't mean you should do it, too. Roles and status of the people engaged in a conversation can differ. Mirroring the physicality of your boss or a potential client, for example, could be interpreted as presumptuous.

Don't try to be the person you're talking to. Be yourself.

3

3.4 Distracting Movements

"But I don't want to distract people with my hands!" is a common refrain. Some speakers shy away from moving at all out of fear of distracting their listeners. Keeping distractions to a minimum is a reasonable goal, but what is it that determines whether a physical movement is distracting?

A distracting movement draws the eye. It takes listeners away from what you are saying. But why?

It has to do with the relationship between your movement and what you're saying. Is the movement in the flow of the expression of your ideas?

A gesture need not have a literal relationship to your words, like pointing up or down. But once an activity leaves the flow—like fiddling with a ring, tapping your fingers, or even pacing—it becomes an independent activity, unrelated to the rest of what's going on. It becomes an eddy in the flow of your ideas that distracts your listeners from your message.

If while you are speaking you realize that some movement of yours has gone rogue and become distracting, you can just stop it, breathe, and free yourself to respond to your more connected and expressive impulses to move.

As long as you are in the flow, let it rip. You will not be distracting; you will be expressive. You will be yourself.

3.5 Sitting vs. Standing

In some circumstances, you will need to be seated when presenting your ideas; in others, you will need to stand. There may also be times when you will have a choice between the two.

When making that choice, avoid the common misconception that sitting is for conversations, while standing is for formal presentations. You can strike a conversational tone whether you are sitting or standing.

But sitters beware! Sitting can imperil your presentation by introducing a variety of hazards that are absent when you are standing. For example, leaning back in your chair can signal a lack of urgency or interest.

Leaning on the table in front of you can affect your posture by rounding your shoulders and can send your focus downward instead of out toward your audience.

A podium, too, can demand to be gripped and leaned upon, limiting your expressiveness and causing you to slouch.

Don't let furniture define your physical presence. A chair, for example, wants to bend you to its will. It was made to hold you up. If you allow a chair to do its job too fully, you may end up draped across it like a clock in a Dalí painting. And even if things don't go that far, the chair may still try to ease you into a slump, draining your energy down and away into the seat and back of the chair.

Can anything be done? Yes!

First of all, when you are sitting, sit toward the front edge of your chair. Chair backs are a primary cause of sitters' slumping. If you aren't touching the chair back, you'll be less likely to try to lean on it.

Now engage your core and hold yourself up, as if you were standing. Stay loose. Keep your hands available and free to jump into action. This will generally mean leaving them where they can be seen. Avoid clasping them, which can close you off and make your hands less likely to participate.

When you are seated at a table, there is less of you visible, which makes it all the more important to bring vitality to what is visible. But pay attention to your under-the-table parts, too.

Check in with your foundation and keep yourself grounded. This matters for two primary reasons:

1. What you do with your legs will affect your upper body posture.
2. What you experience in your own body, regardless of what anyone else can see, will be influenced by the stability of your foundation.

As when you are standing, there is a feeling of readiness and strength that comes from being grounded and balanced.

If you want to cross your legs, you can still have one foot firmly planted rather than leaving them both unstable.

Objects on the table present another set of challenges. They will call out to you, "Play with me!" Don't listen to them. Twirling a pen or fiddling with a water bottle will distract your listeners. Pay attention to your watch, bracelets, cufflinks, or rings; they can become percussive distractions as they hit the tabletop again and again.

Furthermore, sitting can limit your range of motion. If you're at a table, try backing your chair away a few inches to give your upper body some space to move. Backing away from the table a bit can also facilitate eye contact with people seated on either side of you.

It can be hard to look at every person around a table when all of you are seated—do it anyway. Make the effort, turning your head or leaning forward as needed, to specifically include each of your listeners. Choosing a seat with good sightlines, perhaps at the head of the table, makes this task easier. (See Chapter 4: Eye Contact.)

Finally, don't let your voice sag when you sit. It's harder to support your voice when you're sitting, so pay extra attention. (See Chapter 5: Voice.)

You won't always be able to choose whether to sit or stand. However, if you do stand, you may give yourself more physical freedom and a stronger presence, avoid many presentation pitfalls, and make it easier for your listeners to focus on you and your ideas.

✎ Notes from the Workplace ✎

A Boss's Advice

A workshop participant named Harold had been told by his boss that whenever he spoke at a table, he should keep his hands under the table. He had been following that advice.

But by tucking his hands under the table, Harold made himself less visible; he made himself smaller. He also curtailed his ability to express himself physically, which further diminished his presence in the room.

His fellow workshop participants vigorously disagreed with his boss's advice.

I encouraged Harold to free his hands and let us see them while he spoke. He tried it, and we immediately saw more of his personality as well.

There was more Harold in the room!

Beware of bad advice, even from your boss.

A Teacher's Advice

During another workshop, a middle-aged man named Jim sat on his hands as he gave a talk to the group. I asked him about it, and he said that when he was a child, a strict teacher had told him not to move his hands while he spoke. It had stuck with him ever since.

He tried his talk again, but this time he released his hands, allowing them to do whatever they wanted to do. Jim came to life. He became more expressive and more present.

There was more Jim in the room!

Beware of bad advice, even from a teacher.

3.6 The Approach

Consider the moments leading up to a typical standing presentation. The speaker moves toward the front of the room and prepares to address the listeners. Let's call this initial activity "the approach."

Many presenters make no distinction between their approach and their opening words. They begin speaking before they have established their presence and before the audience is ready to listen, weakening the beginning. For the strongest start, distinguish the approach from your content.

The approach has several components, none of which has anything to do with words:

1: Getting Where You Need to Go

Your destination may be a podium, or it may just be a spot where you will be visible to your listeners. The objective here is simple: get there. You don't need to rush to address your audience. You don't even necessarily need to look at them as you are walking. Focus simply on getting where you need to go, and do it with confidence.

2: Claiming Your Space

Once you have arrived at your spot, claim it. Make sure you are balanced and your posture is strong.

3: Connecting with Your Audience

Look at your listeners, make eye contact, and see whether they are ready to give you their attention. If they aren't ready, wait until they are. In some cases, you may need to let them know it's time to begin. Similarly, if you are about to speak from a seated position, take a moment to look around and connect with your audience.

Then start with your content. If you begin your talk prematurely, the power of your initial words may be diminished.

3.7 Smiling

A smile suggests that there is something good going on, that the smiler is appreciating the moment. This appreciation might be about the content or even just about the fact that the communication is happening. In any case, a smile can draw people in and predispose them to listening.

Tap into what's good about your ideas and how they're benefiting your listeners. When you do, a smile is likely to appear on your face, freely, if you let it.

Look for genuine reasons to smile, to appreciate the moment. Leave yourself open to experiencing the positive aspects of what's going on. There is almost always *something* positive you can connect to.

Smiling is great—if you mean it. Forced smiles, on the other hand, are truly off-putting. They seem orchestrated and false. They will make your audience recoil. Your connection with them will suffer. If you don't feel it, don't fake it. A fake smile is creepy and will not serve you or your listeners.

3.8 Handshakes

Many presentation situations begin and end with handshakes. A handshake is a simple thing, but doing it well can make a big difference in the first and last moments of an interaction.

Let's break it down.

The Extension

As you approach your handshake counterpart, extend your (typically right) hand forward at roughly elbow level of your counterpart. Making eye contact is a good idea in this phase, but take a moment to look down so your hands meet smoothly. If neither of you is paying attention, you can have an awkward misplacement.

Calibrate the extension of your arm so your hands meet roughly in the middle of the space between you. Avoid overextending and invading the other person's space. Also avoid underextending and forcing your counterpart to reach too far into your space.

The Grasp

Once your hands have found each other, it's time for the grasp. Don't rush it. If you squeeze down too soon, you run the risk of catching your counterpart's fingers, instead of his or her palm—a distinctly unsatisfying experience for both parties.

Take your time. Allow your palms to meet and settle in at the crook between thumb and forefinger. This won't take long, probably just a moment. But pausing for that moment before squeezing will give your hands a chance to fully embrace, which will strengthen the feeling of connection between you and your handshake counterpart.

Once you do squeeze, give it enough strength so your presence is really felt. A limp hand suggests a limp commitment to the interaction.

But don't go too far in the other direction. Some people try to use handshakes to prove how strong they are, and they squeeze as hard as possible. Others try to pull their handshake counterparts off balance and into their own space.

A handshake is not a contest.

You have the opportunity with a handshake to establish a constructive connection with another person. Make good use of it.

The Release

How long should you squeeze? Long enough to feel like you mean it, but not so long that it gets weird. Figuring out when to release is similar to gauging when eye contact becomes staring. Exercise your own judgment. Pay attention to the other person. Different situations will call for varying squeeze durations.

Fluids

When you wash your hands at work, dry them thoroughly. Coming out of the bathroom and saying "Don't worry; it's just water" is not the best start to a handshake. Similarly, if you put lotion on your hands, rub it in fully, so you don't offer anyone a slimy grip.

3

Chapter 4

4

Eye Contact

Making eye contact with your listeners establishes a connection with them. It conveys sincerity and confidence and keeps you in touch with how they are receiving your ideas. Eye contact is central to an effective in-person presentation.

4.1 Personal Connection

Looking someone in the eye establishes a personal connection and makes the communication feel more conversational, like a shared activity. It invites the person to join in considering your ideas. The stronger your personal connection with your listeners, the better the chance that your ideas will reach them.

4.2 Confidence

Looking people in the eye conveys confidence and authority. Avoiding eye contact, on the other hand, can communicate weakness and fear.

It can be stressful to look out at faces focused on you. That's why some people choose to speak to their notes or to their PowerPoint slides. But ignoring the gazes of audience members doesn't make the audience disappear—unless they get so bored that they walk out!

In fact, by avoiding eye contact, you may actually compound whatever uneasiness you are feeling by turning your focus inward. Making eye contact can combat self-consciousness and nervousness by directing your energy outward toward your listeners. They will then feel that you have an interest in them, increasing the likelihood that they will show an interest in you.

4

4.3 Sincerity

Would you buy a car from a salesperson who wouldn't look you in the eye? Would you trust the advice of a colleague who refused to look at you?

For most people, the answer is no. Without eye contact, it is very difficult to establish trust.

Looking your listeners in the eye says, "I believe what I am saying. You can trust me."

4.4 Respect

When you look someone in the eye, you acknowledge that person's presence. It is respectful. It says, "I see you." People appreciate being seen.

4.5 Focus

People's thoughts are less likely to drift elsewhere when you are looking them in the eye. It's akin to your saying, "Hello there. Are you with me?"

4.6 Responsiveness

Not all people will interrupt you to tell you exactly what's on their mind—"Wait, I'm confused" or "I totally disagree!"

But if you look your audience in the eye, really take them in, you will see what's going on. This will equip you to respond to the cues you receive as you receive them.

This responsiveness helps ensure that the communication is as valuable to your listeners (and to you) as possible.

Confusion

If listeners are confused, you need to figure out why and dispel that confusion right away. Don't wait. If you blithely proceed without clarification, you will dramatically increase the likelihood of losing your audience. They may be distracted by the thing they didn't get, annoyed by your lack of clarity, and less able to follow what follows.

Confusion kills.

Skepticism

Unchecked skepticism is a powerful barrier. If you see that people are skeptical, don't let it slide. Don't pretend that it's not happening.

Maybe you know why they are responding that way, so you can set about dispelling their skepticism immediately. Maybe you need to ask them what the problem is. Do what you need to do to address it without delay.

Boredom

If a listener seems disengaged, ask yourself why. Is it your content? Did you misjudge what really matters to your audience? Do you need to change direction? (See 2.8: Flexibility.) Alternatively, is it some aspect of your delivery that needs an adjustment to draw people back in?

It is critical to ask yourself what you can do to re-engage people whose interest seems to be waning or to connect with those who have been giving you no feedback at all. But sometimes what's going on with people has nothing to do with you and is no reflection at all on the value of what you are saying. Keep this in mind as you interpret your listeners' signals. It may well be the case that what you are saying and how you are saying it are just fine. If so, don't let a few recalcitrant listeners undercut your confidence in what you're doing.

4.7 Technique

When you do make eye contact, try not to stare at a single listener. You should also avoid making only general sweeps of the room or rushing from face to face. Take your time and connect with as many people as the situation comfortably allows. Even if you don't make eye contact with a particular member of a large audience, that person will be able to tell—and will appreciate—that you are specifically and personally engaged with the group.

In a smaller gathering, however, you should make eye contact with every listener. By excluding members of a small group, you risk (1) alienating those whom you exclude and (2) distracting those who notice that you are excluding others.

Including everyone in the room also shows confidence and a command of the space. It conveys the sense that your ideas are valuable and need to be heard.

If you are holding notes during a talk and have to refer to them, bring them up high enough that you can glance at them without having to drop your head much. Of course, they shouldn't be so high that they block your face.

When you don't need to refer to your notes, don't. They can have a magnetic effect, drawing your eyes to them just because they're there.

Finally, practice making eye contact. The more accustomed you are to looking people in the eye in your daily life, the more likely you will be to do it during a business presentation.

If you are uneasy looking people in the eye, do it anyway. Get familiar with the feeling of doing it. Over time, it will become more natural for you, and you will become a more engaging communicator.

Life is full of challenges. We are at our best when we face them rather than avoid them.

✎ Notes from the Workplace ✎

Focusing on the Decision Maker

During a workshop, a senior real estate executive named Monica explained to the group her approach to meetings with potential clients. She would try to identify ahead of time who would be in the room and who the primary decision maker would be. That sounded reasonable. Then we played out a scenario to see how a meeting might go.

Monica picked another workshop participant, Bob, to play the primary decision maker. The other four participants around the table played the team reporting to Bob.

We began the meeting. She started off looking at Bob. As she continued her presentation, she kept looking at Bob, barely even acknowledging any of Bob's support team.

I paused the pretend meeting and asked for comments. Bob reported that while he appreciated the eye contact, it was too much and became distracting. He started thinking, "What about everyone else?"

Bob's team members were also distracted but for a different reason. They felt ignored and disrespected. If Bob had turned to them after the meeting to ask what they thought, the feedback wouldn't have been positive.

Monica's conscious decision to zero in on the decision maker had backfired.

If someone is in the room, that person deserves to be included.

⊘ Terrible Tips: Advice to Ignore ⊘

Instead of looking people in the eye, look at their chins or just over their heads.

Pick a spot on the wall in the back of the room and focus on that.

These terrible tips offer eye-contact avoidance strategies for speakers who find it distracting or uncomfortable to look their listeners in the eye.

But these approaches damage the connection between the speaker and listeners and cause both sides of the communication to lose out on the powerful advantages of eye contact covered in this chapter.

Look people in the eye for a count of three or until you determine what color their eyes are, then go to the next person.

This terrible tip takes eye contact, a naturally fluid and varied activity, and makes it mechanical.

If you went out to dinner with a group of friends and started telling them about a great movie you had just seen, what would your eye contact be like? Would you be counting off the seconds as you moved from person to person? Would you be keeping a tally of eye color? Of course not.

You would be telling your story to everyone around the table, looking at each of them as you went, making sure that what you loved about the movie was getting through to them.

The eye contact would flow freely. You might land with one person for a bit longer than another, have a shared moment with another and move on to the next, but everyone would feel included.

In a business setting, the more similar your mode of eye contact is to the way you look at people in your general life, the more genuine and engaging you will be.

4

Chapter 5

Voice

The way you sound when you speak can bring your words to life—or sap them of their power.

5.1 Warming Up Your Voice

As with the rest of your body, your voice will function optimally when it has been prepared for its task. For example, humming scales and drinking some water before your talk can help you sound your best. Whatever warm-up technique you use, make sure your voice is ready for action before your talk begins.

5.2 Projection, Articulation, and Pitch

You need to speak loudly and clearly enough that your audience—even people in the farthest corner of the room—can easily hear and understand what you are saying. You should also speak at whatever pitch is naturally expressive for you.

We all have a limited capacity for work. The more your listeners have to strain to get your message into their brains, the less energy they have left over to consider it once it's there.

Help make it easy for your audience to receive your ideas by projecting your voice fully and articulating your words with precision.

This will also suggest that what you are saying matters, that you believe it, and that you care enough about it to put some effort into making sure your listeners get it.

The focus of such a delivery is outward. You are launching your message into the room to land squarely with each listener, rather than just letting it dribble out of your mouth.

Projecting your voice also sends more of your personality into the room and more fully shows your relationship to the content.

5

A strong voice conveys confidence. Speaking too softly or mumbling can suggest uncertainty or timidity and will undercut the strength of a presentation. If you're not sure a word or phrase is worth saying, don't say it. If it is worth saying, say it like you mean it.

It's a very common vocal pattern to have volume trail off at the end of a sentence, including at the very end of a presentation. But the words at the end of a sentence still deserve to be heard, unless you decide otherwise, in which case end the sentence earlier.

Some speakers let their voices sag into a grumbly lower register out of laziness or habit. Others force their voices lower in an effort to sound more professional. Either way, these speakers' voices lose energy and expressiveness. Support your voice at its natural pitch, so you can express yourself fully and freely.

If you are using a microphone, keep in mind that while the microphone may add decibels, it cannot give your voice vitality or personality. You need to bring that yourself.

✎ Notes from the Workplace ✎

Fear of Being Too Loud

I have encountered countless people over the years who were afraid of being too loud, but barely any who actually were.

Frequently in my workshops, soft-spoken people stretch themselves, against every instinct, to raise their voices. They can feel embarrassed after doing this, convinced that they were yelling. When this happens, the rest of the group nearly always chimes in to say no, it was not yelling at all—that in fact it could have been louder!

This is one of the most common scenes to play out in my sessions. So many people feel as though they are louder than they are.

What about the people who actually are too loud? They exist, of course, but there are very, very few of them compared to the vast number of people who shy away from using their full and natural voices out of concern for being too loud.

The likelihood that you will accidentally start yelling in the middle of a meeting if you're not careful is effectively zero.

Open up your voice! Let yourself be heard!

⊘ Terrible Tips: Advice to Ignore ⊘

Speak softly so people really have to pay attention.

From time to time, people explain to me that speaking softly is a good way to draw listeners in and make them focus. It's true that volume variety can be interesting. But a sustained period of diminished volume will force listeners to work too hard. After a while (it won't take long), the low talking will become annoying, and listeners will turn their attention to dinner plans or cloud formations.

5

5.3 Pace

When readers want to reread a sentence or paragraph, they can easily do that. Listeners have no such luxury, so the speaker bears responsibility for maintaining a pace that allows the audience time to digest the content. Such a pace also gives the speaker time to think about what he or she is saying and to maintain a meaningful connection to the content.

A speedy pace can suggest that a speaker wants to finish as fast as possible in order to get the whole experience over with. Rushing can also give a sense that the speaker is not very confident about the content and is trying to get through it without having to answer any questions.

Nervous energy often speeds speakers up. If you feel nervous, take a deep breath. Slow down. Keep in mind that what feels slow to you in that moment won't feel slow to anyone else.

5.4 Variety

Variations in tone, pace, and volume occur naturally for a relaxed and engaged speaker. They illustrate the speaker's connection to what he or she is saying, helping the audience to connect as well. Variety also simply makes the words more interesting to hear.

If you have ever had to listen to someone speak in a monotone, you may well have drifted off into your own thoughts. It is no coincidence that the word *monotonous* can mean not only (1) lacking variation in pitch but also (2) boring.

5.5 Inflection and Oral Punctuation

A common problem for speakers involves inflection (change in pitch) at the ends of sentences. Inflection is typically different for questions than for statements. For example, if you answered the phone and didn't hear anyone on the other end right away, but thought it could be Sarah, you might say, "Sarah?" This would be a question; the pitch at the end of "Sarah" would be higher than at the beginning. However, if someone were to ask Sarah her name, she would reply, "Sarah." This would be a statement; the pitch would go down at the end of "Sarah." Say it both ways and listen to the difference.

Some speakers use inflections typically associated with questions when they are actually trying to make statements. This is known as uptalk and can sound tentative or unsure.

For example, if Benjamin said, "My name is Benjamin?" with an upward inflection, he would sound as though he were asking a question. But unless Benjamin has some serious issues, he's not actually asking that question. It just sounds timid.

What other piece of punctuation can be suggested by an upward inflection? A comma.

A comma says, "But wait, there's more." It indicates that the speaker has not yet concluded the current train of thought. Upward inflections at the ends of sentences can act as oral commas, stringing together ideas that should in fact be distinct.

When you indicate with an oral comma that there is more to come, you redirect attention from what you just said to the next thing. You are telling your listeners that you are moving on, which can diminish the importance of where you just were.

A downward inflection, on the other hand—the spoken equivalent of a period—indicates that you are finished with that thought. The thought is standing on its own, not leaning on the next thing. You are inviting your listeners to consider it without the immediate distraction of what's coming next.

It's also easier to pause after a period than after a comma. The more opportunities you give yourself for comfortable pauses, the more flexibility you will have in your delivery.

5.6 Silence

Silence is powerful.

Whether you use it to focus the audience before the first words of a presentation or for emphasis after an important phrase, silence can be extremely effective.

Silence conveys confidence. It tells listeners that the speaker does not feel compelled to fill space with sound in order to justify using their time.

The impulse to avoid silence is hard to ignore—and often leads to the proliferation of fillers such as *um* or *uh*. Fight the impulse. Such fillers can quickly drain energy from a talk and can suggest a lack of confidence.

When you don't know what you want to say next, simply pause; when your next idea comes to you, continue speaking. While a second may feel like an eternity to a speaker searching for the next words, to the audience it really is just a second.

Pauses can bring a sense of thoughtfulness to a talk. A speaker who delivers a perfectly memorized and recited presentation with no moments of searching can actually seem less connected to the content, which will in turn be less engaging for listeners.

Pausing also gives you a chance to breathe. Breathing is good.

5.7 Breathing

Without breath, there is no voice. Timid breathing can support only timid speaking. In contrast, deep, relaxed breathing provides a foundation for a strong, flexible speaking style.

Don't be shy about taking a full breath; everyone needs to breathe. By having enough air, you will have more choices about when to take your next breath, and you can avoid gasping mid-sentence or trailing off at the end of a thought.

Focus on breathing from your diaphragm. Feel your abdomen expand as you inhale and contract as you exhale. This area is the control center for your breath.

5.8 Accents

People who speak English as a foreign language or who grew up in particular regions of the United

States sometimes feel as though their accents get in the way. They may even wish they didn't have them. But accents are part of what makes people who they are, what makes them interesting.

Of course, if a speaker's accent is strong enough that listeners must work to figure out what the speaker is saying, it makes sense for the speaker to try to reduce it. But often when listeners have trouble understanding, it has less to do with a speaker's accent and more to do with the speaker's pace and enunciation. Simply slowing down and enunciating more precisely, whether or not you have an accent, can resolve many of the obstacles to listeners' understanding.

✎ Notes from the Workplace ✎

English as a Foreign Language

During a workshop, an international marketing executive named Maria was addressing her fellow participants. She spoke English quite well but not as her first language. (In fact, it was her third!) She told the group how worried she was that her accent and her occasional grammatical errors were keeping her ideas from reaching her listeners.

It bothered Maria that her speech was different from a typical American's and that it was sometimes imperfect.

But it didn't bother anyone else!

In fact, her own unique way of speaking brought her ideas to life in a vivid, intriguing way. We could understand her perfectly well. Her ideas were clear, but she also gave us something more: an individuality that drew us in.

5

Chapter 6

Nervousness, Confidence, and Imperfection

6

I f you feel nervous about speaking in front of others, you are not alone. Many speakers feel butterflies when all eyes turn to them—but that doesn't mean they aren't confident.

6.1 Your Perspective

What is your perspective on the activity of giving a presentation? What do you perceive to be the expectations of your audience?

In the minds of many anxious speakers, there is a divide that separates them from their listeners. Some speakers feel as though they are performing on their own while the audience listens in. It can be a solitary, even lonely, experience.

If, however, you think of a presentation more as sharing than performing, then in your mind your listeners become more a part of what you're doing, and your presentation becomes a more relaxing and natural experience.

Remind yourself that your listeners don't care about your being perfect. They care about good ideas coming from a genuine, expressive person who has thought about what they need. (See 1.2: Authenticity vs. Professionalism.)

✎ Notes from the Workplace ✎

Speaking to the Boss

"But she's the boss. I need to respect that in the way I communicate with her." This perspective, or one similar to it, is common. Of course, respecting your boss is a good idea. But being overly deferential won't benefit either of you.

If she's a good boss, she's not looking for obsequious employees. She wants smart people with the courage to say out loud what needs to be said, to challenge her ideas, defend their own, and bring a strength to their interactions that says they belong in the room and need to be heard.

Respect is great, but being respectful and being servile are two different things. Don't diminish yourself in the presence of people senior to you.

6.2 What Is Nervousness?

Nervousness is natural. When you are performing an activity that has the potential to, say, land a major new client for your firm, motivate your team at an important juncture, or simply affect your reputation, the stakes are high. Feeling pressure on such occasions is normal and healthy.

Many people would rather never feel nervous again. But eliminating nervousness altogether (non-pharmacologically) is generally not possible. Even if it were possible, it would be a bad idea.

Nervousness is energy.

It gives us a spark, an edge, a focus we wouldn't have without it. This energy arrives for us just when we need it most, just when we are standing or sitting up to say or do something that matters.

You can't keep this energy from arriving. But what you can do is consider how you receive it when it does arrive. Instead of "Oh no, here it comes," how about "Well all right, bring it," recognizing that it is there to serve you, not undermine you.

Of course, a surge of nervous energy has physical effects as the adrenaline flows, so you need to check in with your body.

Are your shoulders tight? Are your hands clenched? Release them.

Has your breathing become shallow? Take a slow, deep breath.

Think of the people you may have seen step up to shoot a free throw with no time left on the clock, set up for a game-winning penalty kick, or get ready to serve for the match. What do they all do before they take that shot, kick that ball, or swing that racket at that crucial moment?

They take a deep breath. They check in with their bodies and loosen up. Maybe they bounce a bit, shake out their arms, or roll their shoulders.

Do you think they don't feel nervous? Do you

think they don't feel that surge of energy? Of course they feel it. But they do what they need to do to allow that energy to flow freely through them into the task at hand. They let that energy strengthen their performance. They stay focused on what matters.

✎ Notes from the Workplace ✎

Maintaining Your Focus

When I was 25 years old, I spent a summer playing basketball on tour against the Harlem Globetrotters. One day we were in a stadium somewhere in the middle of Europe. I had just been fouled on a shot, and I was heading to the free-throw line. The referee handed me the ball. All eyes in the stadium were on me.

Free throws were a big deal to me. I hated it whenever I missed one. It seemed as though there was just no excuse for missing. No one is defending you. All you need to do is stand there, all alone, and make the shot.

There I stood, all alone, ball in hand. I felt the pressure of the thousands of expectant faces. I took a deep breath, wiggled a bit, focused on the hoop, brought the ball up in front of me, bent my knees, and...

At that very moment, a Globetrotter who had snuck up behind me grabbed my shorts and yanked them down. It all happened so quickly. As you might imagine, I had never prepared for such a scenario.

6

But there I was. And I was there to make a free throw. With my shorts suddenly down around my knees, I stayed focused on what really mattered and followed through with the shot.

It went in. I pulled up my shorts. The crowd went wild.

6.3 Preparation

Preparation is perhaps the single most powerful antidote to excessive nervousness. The more prepared you are, the more confidence you will have in yourself, which will in turn inspire your listeners' confidence in you.

While preparation is critical, avoid memorizing your entire talk or writing out every word of a speech and reading it to your audience. Focusing too much on the specific order of your words as you speak, rather than on the flow of your ideas, can prevent you from having a more natural connection to your content.

However, you should memorize the opening words—perhaps the first sentence or so—of your presentation and practice this beginning segment repeatedly. You can boost your confidence by minimizing any worry about bungling your first words.

When you know that your beginning will go well, you can direct your energy outward, toward the audience, connecting with them instead of focusing inward. A strong opening to your presentation will establish a confident tone and launch you powerfully into the rest of your talk.

To help keep your talk on track, you may wish to have some brief notes with you to remind you of your key points. These notes should be spare and very legible so that with a quick glance, you can get what you need and return your focus to your listeners. (See 8.1: Categories of Presentation Materials.)

In addition to preparing your content, consider the setting for your talk. Will you be in a colleague's office? A boardroom or conference room? A banquet hall? Experienced presenters often visit the space where they will be speaking in order to familiarize themselves with it in advance of a talk. Many athletes, too, will visit the site of an upcoming competition so that they can walk the court or field and get a sense of the venue before competing there. If your surroundings are familiar, you will feel more comfortable.

Prepare your body, too. (See 3.2: Physical Warm-Up Exercises.)

6

✎ Notes from the Workplace ✎

Speaking Up in Meetings

I was coaching Louise, a senior vice president of a global manufacturing company. She explained that she was finding it difficult to make her points during her firm's executive committee meetings.

The rest of the committee members seemed perfectly willing to chime in with ideas that were not yet fully formed. She was inclined, however, to give more thought to an idea before saying it out loud. Often by the time she was ready to speak, the conversation had moved on.

To Louise, words really mattered. She wanted to be sure to make the best possible use of everyone's time when she did decide to speak. But part of making good use of people's time is getting them the ideas they need at the right time.

In the back-and-forth of a meeting, this sometimes means sharing ideas before you have had a chance to prepare them as thoroughly as you would have liked. This can feel a bit risky.

But playing it too safe can mean that too many good ideas in your mind never make it to other people—a bad result for everyone.

You need to balance the intrinsic value of your idea in its current form against your impulse to vet it fully before putting it out there. Sometimes, you just have to take a chance.

6.4 Imperfection

No matter how well you prepare, you will not escape the fact that you are imperfect. Sometime, somewhere, you will make a mistake.

Although you can't eliminate your mistakes altogether, you can choose how you respond to them. In fact, your response will typically define the moment more than the error itself. Instead of fretting when you make a mistake, just correct it if necessary, feel free to laugh if it was funny, and move on.

It's easy to be your own harshest critic when you stumble, turning inward and striking a negative, disappointed, or even apologetic tone. But no one else cares that you aren't perfect. Don't let your mistakes distract you from your message and your connection to your audience.

When you err, be kind to yourself, embrace your imperfection as a part of who you are, and maintain an outward focus on getting your ideas to your listeners.

Spoken language is naturally flawed. We stop in the middle of sentences and backtrack, we choose words that may not fit perfectly in a particular context, and our syntax can be convoluted. Unless you read from a script or recite your talk word for word from memory (not recommended—see the previous section), you may well say something that you wish you had said in other words or not at all.

However, a natural delivery with some mistakes will engage listeners far more than an error-free but flat alternative. In fact, moments of imperfection can be some of the most engaging moments of a presentation. They are real. They are utterly human. Your listeners are human, too.

✎ Notes from the Workplace ✎

Appreciating Yourself

I often ask people at the end of a workshop to give one last presentation to the group about two observations they have made: (1) something they observed about someone else in the workshop that was good, and (2) something about themselves and the way they communicate that is good.

People have an easy time with the first observation. In fact, they often dole out praise to multiple classmates, going from one to the other with specific and encouraging thoughts. But they struggle to come up with something good to say about themselves.

It is a natural impulse for ambitious people with high expectations of themselves to focus on what they want to change and who they want to become. But a significant part of the power you can bring to any interaction comes from embracing who you are already and recognizing your strengths.

Appreciate yourself.

6.5 Relaxation Strategies

If you are feeling overly nervous, try to identify specifically why you feel that way. Are you afraid of certain potential outcomes? What are they, and why do they worry you? Are your fears reasonable? Once you have identified and clarified your concerns, they become targets for solutions.

Nervousness manifests itself not only in your mind, but also in your body. Therefore, use your body as well as your brain to dispel nervousness. Try the exercises outlined in 3.2: Physical Warm-Up Exercises. And don't leave them totally behind when you begin presenting; stay aware of your body and your breathing as you speak so you can avoid tensing up.

In addition, by focusing your thoughts and energy in a productive way before you give your talk, you can bolster your confidence. Remind yourself how well you understand the material and how carefully you have prepared. Think about how fortunate the audience will be to see and hear you.

Remind yourself what your listeners care about—and what they don't. They care about your being genuine and expressive. They care about your understanding them, giving them good ideas, and making really good use of their time. They do not care about your being perfect.

Try visualization, a technique often used by athletes, actors, and musicians in advance of competition or performance. Visualize your presentation from beginning to end. Start with the instant you walk into the room or onto the stage, and think through every moment until you leave the room or return to your seat after your talk.

Be specific. See the room and your listeners' engaged faces; think about the valuable things you are saying and how well they are received. Notice your confident posture, strong and flexible voice, and consistent eye contact. Breathe deeply and calmly as you see yourself deliver the most natural, engaging, valuable presentation you can possibly imagine.

Don't forget that your audience wants you to do well. They are there to hear your message, not to criticize you. They are not anxious about your presentation. Tap into that calming perspective.

Immediately before you give your presentation, clear your mind. Your preparation is over. You are ready. Take a deep breath and be yourself.

⊘ Terrible Tips: Advice to Ignore ⊘

Picture your audience in their underwear.

This terrible tip is meant to impress upon speakers that their audience is human, just like them. That's a reasonable idea to keep in mind. But following this tip literally would probably be more distracting than relaxing. Keep their clothes on.

6

Chapter 7

Questions, Answers, and Listening

Answering people's questions can be one of the most important things you do in a presentation. It shows listeners how well you understand the topic and how responsive you are able to be.

7.1 Preparing for Questions

Preparation is crucial to being able to respond well to questions. When you really know your subject and have thought about the questions people may ask you about it, you can answer more directly and confidently.

In addition to preparing on your own, it can be useful to get your colleagues involved, especially when they are familiar with your content and your audience. Brainstorming with them about what questions might come up can help identify issues you haven't considered. And role-playing questions and answers can prepare you for how the interactions may unfold.

7.2 Listening and Answering

When someone asks a question, listen carefully to what is being asked so you can respond specifically.

Repeating generalities you have already covered in your talk is not likely to satisfy your audience.

Have you ever heard a politician reply to a question without actually addressing what was asked? Unfortunately, such responses are not confined to politics. One sure way to frustrate an audience is to respond to their questions without answering them.

Before you give an answer, make sure all of your listeners have heard the question; repeat it if necessary. If you need clarification, don't hesitate to ask for it.

If you don't know the answer, simply say so, and perhaps offer to call or email the questioner later with the answer or other relevant information.

Admitting that you don't know the answer to a question is far better than guessing. In fact, the audience will appreciate your candor and will be more inclined to trust the answers you do give them.

It's fine not to have an answer for every question. Much as you should embrace your imperfection, you should embrace your non-omniscience. If you seem insecure or apologetic about not knowing, it can shake the audience's confidence in you.

When you do have an answer, keep it concise. Give others a chance to ask their questions, too.

In some situations, you may mostly be just listening. Keep in mind that even in silence, your body language, eye contact, and facial expressions will be sending out many cues about how you are receiving the ideas coming your way.

✎ Notes from the Workplace ✎

Attention to Detail

I often ask workshop participants to pair up, present topics to each other, and then deliver presentations to the rest of the group about their partners' topics.

This is an exercise not only about conveying ideas effectively, but also about listening carefully. Listening well is hard work and requires paying attention to the details. Some participants will present a topic fairly accurately but get one or two elements wrong, distorting key aspects of the topic and changing the tone of the whole talk.

At times, participants also provide their own connections between facts to help a narrative when no such connections actually exist. This, too, can significantly alter the meaning of a talk. Don't do it.

Listen carefully. Value accuracy.

⊘ Terrible Tips: Advice to Ignore ⊘

Never take "no" for an answer.

Presentations often involve some element of persuasion. When you are trying to persuade people, it's important to listen closely and respond appropriately.

Many businesspeople are under the misconception that being aggressive and insistent—and not taking "no" for an answer—is the best path to success. Confidence is a good thing, but flexibility and responsiveness to the people you're trying to persuade are just as important. Listening is a sign of respect. Show respect for "no."

At the heart of *Never take "no" for an answer* is the message "be persistent," which is itself not a bad idea. It's not unreasonable to try to understand the nature of someone's objections so you can address them. But don't let your persistence become badgering. There comes a time to accept what people are saying and respect their wishes, even when they don't align with your own.

There is strength and dignity in that moment of acquiescence, free of the whiff of desperation that can come with not taking "no" for an answer. Accepting "no" without an undue struggle suggests you are not in dire need of this particular "yes," that you are confident in the many other yeses to come.

Perhaps we could modify this terrible tip to make it not so terrible: *Don't let the last "no" keep you from seeking the next "yes."*

7.3 Control

When you are interacting with your listeners, maintaining control of a presentation can be a challenge. However, it is your responsibility to ensure that the interaction does not drift away from a productive focus.

When someone asks you a question, evaluate the

audience. Are they nodding in agreement? Are they rolling their eyes? Are they experts who already know the answer to the question?

Your response will have to balance the needs of the questioner with the needs of the rest of the audience.

Although responding to certain questions can take you away from your intended topic, your listeners may well appreciate your flexibility and willingness to improvise.

However, when a question is asking for a detour that is not best for the group, don't waste time on it. You can offer to speak to the questioner later or recommend another source for the answer. If the person presses you further, don't be shy about making your position clear. You are the steward of *all* of your listeners' time. Don't waste it. (See 2.7: Time.)

Chapter 8

Presentation Materials

Too often, when people sit down to prepare for a presentation, they think first about what PowerPoint slides they should use.

Try thinking instead about your audience, your ideas, and how your themes will unfold. Maybe you don't need slides at all. Add them only where absolutely necessary to clarify or simplify ideas, more fully engage your listeners, or otherwise strengthen a moment of your talk.

Superfluous slides will suck the life out of your presentation.

8.1 Categories of Presentation Materials

There are several types of presentation materials, each with its own audience and purpose. It is certainly possible to give an excellent talk without using any presentation materials at all, but in some cases you may want to use one or more of the following:

Visual Aids

Audience: People listening to you

Purpose: To support you in the delivery of your message. Visual aids should have limited text and should make use of graphical images where appropriate.

Speaker Notes
Audience: You
Purpose: To help you remember to address key points. These notes should be minimal, consisting of the fewest words necessary to remind you of an idea or detail. The font (or handwriting) should be clear and large enough that you can read it very easily.

Handouts Distributed Just Before or During a Talk
Audience: People listening to you
Purpose: To support you in the delivery of your message. Before handing out any materials, consider carefully whether the audience really needs to refer to them, and if so, when. Ill-timed handouts can distract listeners and diminish the strength of your message.

8

Post-Talk Handouts
Audience: People reading the handouts after a talk. These could be people who did not attend the presentation or who did attend but want to be reminded of the specifics later.

Purpose: To enable the readers to understand the presentation you gave without the benefit of having you right there to illuminate the material. These handouts, therefore, can be quite detailed.

Many speakers do not distinguish among these categories in preparing their presentation materials. The results can be disastrous. For example, some presenters convert outlines of their talks (essentially their own speaker notes) into slides and project them while they speak, reading from the screen. Such behavior diverts focus from the speaker and detracts from the spontaneity of the message.

Another common and unfortunate approach is to use detailed documentation (which should really be distributed as a post-talk handout) as a visual aid. The result is a series of high-density slides that can pull attention away from the speaker as the audience tries to decipher what they're looking at. Furthermore, the important messages that the speaker would have liked to convey in such a presentation are often lost in the details.

8.2 When to Use Visual Aids

If you are considering using visual aids (PowerPoint slides, for example), the first question you should ask yourself is whether you really need them at all.

If it is not clear that using visual aids will make you more effective in some specific and significant way, then don't. Be ruthless in your evaluation of potential slides. Get rid of them unless you really, truly need them.

Think of the greatest speakers of all time. They moved us, enlightened us, and compelled us to action; they made us think, laugh, and cry. It was not visual aids that made these speakers effective.

8.3 How to Use Visual Aids

If you decide to incorporate visual aids into your talk, limit your use of text. In addition, keep any text you do use simple and easy to read. Graphical images are particularly well suited to visual aids because they can communicate a lot of information very quickly (charts of data trends, for example). The audience can glance at an image, grasp the concept it illustrates, and immediately turn their attention back to you.

The slide below is dense with data. Since there are so many numbers on the slide, the story that the numbers are telling is not readily apparent.

Projected Revenue Comparison
(in millions)

	Project Starship	Project Scooter	Project Skateboard
Year 1	$75	$204	$325
Year 2	$96	$211	$320
Year 3	$117	$218	$315
Year 4	$138	$225	$310
Year 5	$159	$232	$305
Year 6	$180	$239	$300
Year 7	$201	$246	$295
Year 8	$222	$253	$290
Year 9	$237	$260	$285
Year 10	$252	$267	$280

But a graphical representation of the same data, as seen on the next slide, makes the relative trends of the numbers easy to see.

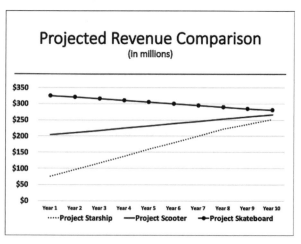

The slide below is dense with text. Too much text distracts the audience from the speaker as they are drawn to read the words. Text-heavy slides that tell the audience everything they need to know can also make the speaker essentially redundant.

How We Address Client Needs

- The process of creating the best solutions for our clients has multiple stages, each of which is very important to the ultimate success of our client relationships.
  - In the first step, we brainstorm about the possible ways we might meet the needs of the client. Creativity is paramount here. There are no bad ideas at this stage. In fact, we encourage people to share whatever comes to mind during these brainstorming sessions.
  - Next, we evaluate the ideas we generated in the first step, select the best ones, and develop them into a client proposal.
  - Finally, we deliver our proposal to the client. Because we have put such creativity and focus into the process, the results are the best they can possibly be. This makes the client very happy.

Some speakers might opt for the more graphical slide below. But even this slide is more than the audience needs to understand such a basic idea.

8

An even simpler alternative to a text-heavy slide:

No slide at all! You could skip the visual aid altogether and just talk about your ideas. This will often be your best choice.

If you do choose to use visual aids, take care not to upstage yourself. If you are projecting PowerPoint slides, for example, place a notebook computer or monitor in front of you (not blocking your face) so you will know what is on the projection screen without having to turn around to look at it. Proper placement of your equipment will help you maintain your connection with the audience, even as you display your slides.

Some people like to sit toward the back of the room at a computer and speak from there as they go through their slides. This makes it much more difficult to maintain a connection with the audience.

Keeping your primary focus on the listeners will help them keep their primary focus on you. Don't let a visual aid break your connection to the audience. It is this connection—not an image on a screen—that is most compelling and that will most contribute to the successful delivery of your message.

8

✎ Notes from the Workplace ✎

A Memorable Misuse of PowerPoint

An advertising agency needed to lay off some employees and was conducting interviews of the staff to help decide whom to let go. I was asked to sit in.

Roland was the senior executive leading the interviews. He and I sat in a conference room awaiting Bruce, the next interviewee. Bruce arrived at the appointed time with a laptop under his arm and shook our hands. He sat down, opened up his computer, and turned it toward us so we could see the screen.

He hit a key and a PowerPoint presentation began. His first slide was the word START in large font. He gave us a moment to process that and proceeded with his second slide, reading aloud the words on the screen: I THINK I'M PRETTY GOOD.

Then the next slide: YOU THINK I'M PRETTY GOOD. Before Roland could respond, Bruce hit us with the slide that brought it all home: COMMON GROUND.

PowerPoint cannot save fundamentally weak content.

But it can leave an indelible memory.

8.4 The Curse of the Agenda

Many speakers begin their presentations by reading through an agenda slide, point by point. "I'll start with this. Then I'll cover that. Then I'll talk about this, and that, and that…" This approach curses their presentations with a perfunctory, unimaginative, even lazy tone from the very start.

It's not easy to come up with an engaging beginning for your talk. Do it anyway. (See 2.3: The Beginning.)

If for some reason you are required to have a slide with an agenda, consider going to it only after you have engaged the audience.

8

Chapter 9

Speaking on the Phone and Related Topics

When you are speaking on the phone, you can't see your listeners, and they can't see you. But a phone call's success still depends on many of the same elements that contribute to the effectiveness of a face-to-face talk. In addition, a phone call poses challenges for a speaker that an in-person communication does not.

9.1 Your Body

What you do with your body matters even when you are on the phone. If you let your body sag while you speak, your energy will sag, and your voice may convey a lack of interest, confidence, or personality. Sit up, or even stand up, to help make a message feel like it matters. (See Chapter 3: Body Language.)

9.2 Your Voice

When you speak on the phone, you send no visual cues, and the clarity of your voice isn't the same as it is in person. Make an extra effort to articulate precisely, slow down, and project your voice. Make it easy for your listeners to get your message.

You also don't *receive* any visual cues over the phone. Reading your listeners' reactions to your ideas can be difficult. You can't see skepticism or enthusiasm on a listener's face; you can't see the raised hand of someone who wants to interject or ask a question.

Try to communicate in a way that invites your listeners to participate, so you know how your message is being received. Speak at a relaxed pace, allow yourself to pause, and ask your listeners periodically if they have any questions or comments.

If a call takes place first thing in the morning before you've talked to anyone, or if it's later on but you haven't spoken in a while, warm up your voice a bit before you pick up the phone so you don't start with a grumble.

Although a phone can transmit the sound of your voice, it can't give your voice the personality and strength that will bring your message to life. That part is up to you. (See Chapter 5: Voice.)

9.3 Placing and Receiving Calls

When you call someone, the first thing you should do is identify yourself. Soon thereafter, let the person know why you are calling. Don't ask for two minutes of someone's time if you really intend to use 10.

When you answer the phone, use a polite tone of

voice. You may be very busy or under stress, but don't take it out on the caller. Also, give your name right away, so that the caller knows immediately whether he or she has reached the right person.

✎ Notes from the Workplace ✎

Cold Callers and "Hi, how are you?"

So many cold callers ask me how I am as soon as I pick up the phone, before they tell me who they are or why they are calling. This approach must feature prominently in someone's call-center handbook.

It may be intended to establish a friendly connection and warm up the person on the other end.

But it fails.

If you are calling strangers, interrupting them in the middle of whatever they are doing, don't pretend to be their friend. Don't try to manipulate them with fake small talk. Tell them who you are and why you are using their time.

9.4 Using a Speakerphone

A speakerphone can be very useful when multiple people in a room need to participate in a call. However, it's typically not as easy for a person on the other end of a call to hear you clearly when you talk into a speakerphone, so if you're alone in your office and don't have a good reason to use one, don't. Instead, pick up your handset or put on your headset. Unnecessary speakerphone use can convey self-importance and a lack of respect for listeners.

When you do use a speakerphone and you have others in the room with you, say so right away. It's not only polite but also ethical to make sure all people on a call know who their audience is.

With a speakerphone, you'll often have two sets of listeners—one set on the other end of the phone and one in the room with you. Avoid hunching over and staring down as you speak. Sit up, project your voice, and look at the other people in the room. (See Chapter 4: Eye Contact.)

If you use the mute button, use it carefully. Confirm that the feature is actually working on your phone by asking, "Can you hear me?" or something similar. Only after you are sure the phone is muted should you say anything you wouldn't want the listeners on the other end to hear.

Even if you're sure your mute feature is activated, be cautious about saying anything that would cause a problem if it were heard by the other call participants. Technology is imperfect, and buttons get bumped.

9.5 Conference Calls

A conference call may or may not involve speakerphones, but it does involve multiple participants. As participants multiply, so do the challenges to efficient, clear communication.

If listeners might not know it's you, identify yourself as you begin to speak. This applies to the first time you speak and also to your subsequent comments. Of course, if you are the only woman in a group of men or vice versa, people probably won't have much trouble knowing when it's you speaking.

Avoid speaking over another person. It is rude, and you may both have to repeat yourselves, wasting everyone's time.

Also, listen! It can be much more difficult to pay attention when the person speaking is not in the room with you. Do it anyway.

When you are on a conference call, avoid typing or making other tapping sounds, and keep your electronic devices from beeping, ringing, or audibly vibrating. These noises can distract listeners and suggest that your focus is not on the conversation at hand.

9.6 Videoconference Calls

During a videoconference call, you need to pay attention not only to the people on the screen but also to the camera that's pointed at you.

When you look into the camera, the people you're speaking to will feel as though you are looking at them. But you will feel as though you are looking into a camera, and you will be less able to pick up on how your audience is responding.

On the other hand, when you look at the people on your screen, you will feel more connected, but it may appear to them as though you are looking somewhere else.

Balance your points of visual focus so you know what's going on with your audience but you also give them some virtual eye contact.

9.7 Your Outgoing Voicemail Greeting

Your outgoing voicemail greeting conveys not only practical information but also an impression—sometimes a first impression—of who you are. Make your greeting clear, concise, and polite; support your voice with energy and personality.

Limit the information in your greeting to what

9

callers really need to know. Give your first and last name, and perhaps your company's name and department, so callers know that they have reached you and not someone else. You may want to thank them for calling, invite them to leave a message, and say that you will call back. If you know you won't call back promptly (because of vacation or some other reason), you should say so and perhaps give the number of a colleague to call in your absence. If your specific situation requires any more information, add it sparingly.

In addition, make your greeting accurate and keep it current. If you leave the office at 5:00 p.m., people who call you at 5:30 p.m. shouldn't get a greeting that says, "I am in the office but unable to answer the phone." If it's Wednesday, don't keep the greeting you had the day before about being at an off-site meeting all day Tuesday. An erroneous voicemail greeting is unprofessional and may be confusing and annoying for callers.

9.8 Leaving Voicemail Messages

Before you pick up the phone to make a call, remind yourself that you might reach voicemail instead of a person. Try to picture the recipient of your call as he or she plays your message. What would make especially good use of the recipient's time? What would make it as easy as possible for the person to understand and act on your message?

Speak clearly and don't rush. Voice recordings are generally not as easy to understand as the real thing.

Say as little as possible to get your idea across. Yours will probably not be the only message your listener receives that day; respect your listener's time. If voicemail systems frequently cut you off before you have finished, you are saying too much.

Unless you are certain that the person you are calling knows your phone number by heart, include it in your message. Doing so makes it easier for the person to call you back and more likely that you will get a prompt return call. Also, say your number early in the message (and slowly) so that if the recipient needs to replay your message to confirm your number, it won't be necessary to listen to the whole thing again.

9.9 Engaging with the People Around You

Some people walk around the workplace and ride the elevators with their eyes glued to their phones, oblivious to the people around them. When they do this, they miss out on myriad potential human connections: smiles, hellos, and other simple moments of mutual acknowledgment.

These interactions, as brief as they are, help build relationships and establish people's presence in the workplace.

When you are walking about, put your phone away and leave yourself open to connecting with the people around you.

✎ Notes from the Workplace ✎

Leaving Technology Behind

I worked with a group of technology professionals at an international bank who were responsible for protecting the firm from cyberattacks. They were accustomed to having their phones with them and active at all times. They would even sleep with them nearby and reply to messages at all hours of the night.

For our full-day workshop, the group arranged, remarkably, to be without their devices. It was rough going at first, as device separation anxiety set in. But before long, unease gave way to relief, and they were very happy about being able to devote their full attention to what was happening right in front of them.

Try going device-free yourself for a day, or even part of a day. You might like it, too.

Device Addiction

My workshops are device-free zones. I ask people to put away their phones and other devices so they can be fully present. Nonetheless, in the midst of one session, a participant named Alex furtively checked his phone in a quick grasp-lift-swipe-look-replace maneuver as I was mid-sentence. I paused and asked him about it.

He apologized and assured me that his phone was off, as it had been since the beginning of the class.

He sheepishly explained that it hadn't been a conscious decision to check his phone. He had done it out of habit, even though his phone was off.

Be aware of your habits.

Beware of your phone.

Self-Importance

A participant in one of my workshops, a financial executive named Tom, said that he thought looking at his phone during meetings made him seem important, as though he had a lot going on.

The rest of the group objected and said that such behavior actually made Tom look disrespectful and disengaged. Tom got the message.

Leaving your phone shut off in your bag or in your pocket shows respect for the people you are with. There is also a strength that comes from being in command of your own time, not allowing yourself to be buffeted by random buzzes and beeps that try to pull you away from what you're doing.

When you are meeting with people in person, unless you are in the middle of an emergency that requires you to have your phone out (in which case you should tell them that you are in the middle of an emergency that requires you to have your phone out), put it away.

Focus on the people in front of you.

9

Chapter 10

Taking Advice

Over the course of your life so far, you have certainly received solicited and unsolicited advice from a broad array of people—some of it, perhaps, concerning your way of communicating.

You will continue to receive all sorts of supposed words of wisdom. When you do, exercise your own judgment, vigorously, rather than reflexively accepting any recommendations. Ask yourself whether the advice you are being given rings true. Does it fit with who you are? Will adopting it really contribute to your positive development?

And consider the source. Who is giving you the advice? Why are they doing it? What personal bias may be affecting their perspective?

Feedback can be great. But blindly accepting unfounded criticism can be crippling.

Beware of bad advice.

Conclusion

Awareness! Practice!

Open your eyes and your ears to the endless flow of communication around you. Think about what you appreciate, what seems effective, what seems less so, and why. Consider what elements of your own way of communicating seem to influence people's appreciation of you and your ideas.

As you read the final pages of this book, you may be thinking ahead, eager to put to work what you have learned. Fortunately, there are infinite opportunities to practice. You don't need to wait until your next big business meeting or keynote address. Practice when you're out to dinner with friends, when you're at home with your family, when a stranger asks you for directions, or when you're checking out at the grocery store. Practice when you speak to your neighbors or your taxi driver. Practice when you call for tech support for your latest gadget. The more accustomed you are to communicating effectively in your personal life, the more likely you will be to communicate effectively when your business success depends on it.

As you develop your awareness and keep on practicing, it is essential that you focus not only on the things you may want to change but also on the things you already do well. Every person has positive elements of his or her communication style.

When you walk into a room, pick up a phone, step up to a podium, or take your seat at a table, remind yourself of the wonderful aspects of the way you communicate. Tap into that well of positive energy and be yourself.

Appendix

Checklists

Authenticity

- ☐ Be yourself.
- ☐ Tell the truth.

Content

- ☐ Know your audience.
- ☐ Know your objectives.
- ☐ Understand your topic well and find something in it that matters to you.
- ☐ Engage your audience immediately.
- ☐ Organize your talk logically, making it easy to follow.
- ☐ Clarify your ideas with specifics and examples.
- ☐ Avoid jargon.
- ☐ If you can say something in fewer words, do.
- ☐ Stay flexible and responsive to your listeners' needs.
- ☐ Use language that is natural to your speaking style.
- ☐ Make good use of your listeners' time.
- ☐ In your conclusion, emphasize what matters most, and tell your listeners if you want them to do something.

Body Language

☐ Warm up and stretch out.

☐ Remember that you begin communicating with your audience as soon as you become visible to them.

☐ Maintain an upright and relaxed posture.

☐ Stay balanced.

☐ Breathe.

☐ Leave your hands available.

☐ Stay open to your natural impulses to move.

☐ Avoid pacing, pen tapping, handwringing, and other distractions.

☐ Don't let furniture define your physical presence.

☐ When you have a choice, consider standing rather than sitting.

☐ Before you begin speaking, (1) get where you need to go, (2) claim your space, and (3) connect with your audience.

☐ Consider what's positive about your presentation and allow yourself to smile.

☐ Pay attention when you shake people's hands.

Eye Contact

- ☐ Look your listeners in the eye.
- ☐ Avoid making only general sweeps of the audience, staring, or rushing from one face to the next.
- ☐ Allow your eye contact to be natural and varied.
- ☐ Read your audience's responses and react accordingly.
- ☐ If you need to refer to notes you are holding, hold them up high enough that you can glance at them without having to drop your head much.
- ☐ When you don't need to refer to notes, don't.
- ☐ Practice making eye contact in your daily life.

Voice

- ☐ Warm up your voice.
- ☐ Speak loudly enough that the people in the back of the room can hear you well.
- ☐ Articulate so that your words are easily understood.
- ☐ Support your voice at its natural pitch.
- ☐ Speak at a pace that makes it easy for your listeners to follow what you are saying.
- ☐ If something is worth saying, then say it like you mean it.
- ☐ Vary your tone, pace, and volume.
- ☐ In general, use upward inflections for questions or to connect ideas, and use downward inflections for statements.
- ☐ Remember that silence is powerful.
- ☐ Avoid fillers such as *um* or *uh*.
- ☐ Breathe deeply and freely.

Nervousness, Confidence, and Imperfection

- ☐ Remind yourself that your listeners do not care about your being perfect and that they want you to do well.
- ☐ Nervousness is energy. Use it to fuel your presentation.
- ☐ Prepare.
- ☐ Memorize the first words of your talk.
- ☐ If possible, familiarize yourself with the setting of your presentation.
- ☐ Focus on your strengths.
- ☐ Visualize your presentation's success.
- ☐ Loosen up and stretch out. Stay loose.
- ☐ Breathe.
- ☐ Don't fret over mistakes. Embrace your imperfection.
- ☐ Be yourself!

Questions, Answers, and Listening

- ☐ Anticipate possible questions and prepare answers to them in advance of your presentation.
- ☐ Listen carefully. Pay attention to details.
- ☐ When asked a question, respond specifically to what is being asked.
- ☐ Ask for clarification if you need it.
- ☐ Before you give an answer, make sure all of your listeners have heard the question. Repeat the question if necessary.
- ☐ If you don't know the answer to a question, say so.
- ☐ Be concise.
- ☐ When you are trying to persuade people, be responsive to what they say and don't push too hard.
- ☐ When answering a question, keep in mind the interests and needs of the entire audience, not just the questioner.

Presentation Materials

- ☐ Ask yourself whether you really need visual aids at all. If you don't need them, don't use them.
- ☐ Remember that visual aids, speaker notes, and handouts all have different forms and functions.
- ☐ Limit text in visual aids. If you do include text, keep it simple and easy to read.
- ☐ Make use of graphical images in visual aids, where appropriate.
- ☐ Do not allow your visual aids or handouts to upstage you.
- ☐ If you use speaker notes, make sure they are very concise and easy for you to read.
- ☐ Maintain your connection to the audience. You should be their primary focus, and they should be yours.
- ☐ Avoid using agenda slides whenever possible.

Speaking on the Phone and Related Topics

- ☐ Remember that posture matters, even on the phone.
- ☐ Pay extra attention to speaking clearly without rushing.
- ☐ Identify yourself as necessary.
- ☐ Avoid using a speakerphone when you don't have to.
- ☐ When using a speakerphone, tell your listeners if anyone else is in the room with you.
- ☐ If you use the mute button, use it carefully.
- ☐ On a conference call, listen attentively, avoid talking over people, and don't make distracting noises.
- ☐ On a videoconference call, remember that what feels like eye contact to you may not feel like it to the people on the other end.
- ☐ Make your outgoing voicemail greeting clear, concise, and polite. It should also be accurate and current.
- ☐ When leaving a voicemail message, keep it brief and include your phone number (early in the message), unless the recipient knows it by heart.
- ☐ Put your phone away when you can, and engage with the people around you.

Taking Advice

☐ Beware of bad advice.

About the Author

Brandt Johnson is a co-founder and principal of Syntaxis, a communication skills training firm based in New York City. A former investment banker and speechwriter, Brandt has conducted presentation skills training for executives at major organizations across the United States. He is also a playwright, actor, and lifelong athlete who played professional basketball in Europe and on tour against the Harlem Globetrotters. Brandt graduated from Williams College with a BA in mathematics and has an MBA in finance from the NYU Stern School of Business. He lives in Manhattan with his wife, Ellen Jovin.

About Syntaxis

Syntaxis is a communication skills training firm based in New York City. The company was founded in 1999 by the author of this book, Brandt Johnson, and his wife, Ellen Jovin.

Through workshops and one-on-one coaching, Syntaxis helps people at all stages of their careers, from new hires to CEOs, to communicate with greater clarity, authenticity, and power.

Subject areas include presentation skills, executive presence, pitch preparation, grammar, business writing, email etiquette, editing, and English as a foreign language. All Syntaxis training is delivered by one of the two founders, either Brandt or Ellen. Brandt conducts the training in presentation skills and executive presence, while Ellen conducts the training in written communication skills.

Syntaxis clients include many of the world's leading corporations.

For more information, please visit syntaxis.com.

Index